The American Indian Wars

Explore the Conflict and Tragedy from Beginning to End

Brent Schulte, **History** Compacted

Copyright © 2019 by Sea Vision Publishing

All Rights Reserved.

No part of this publication may be reproduced, distributed, or transmitted in any form or by any means, including photocopying, recording, electronic or mechanical methods, without the prior written permission of the publisher, except in the case of brief quotations embodied in critical reviews and certain other non-commercial uses permitted by copyright law.

Much research, from a variety of sources, has gone into the compilation of this material. We strive to keep the information up-to-date to the best knowledge of the author and publisher; the materials contained herein is factually correct. Neither the publisher nor author will be held responsible for any inaccuracies.

ISBN: 9781699010990

Table of Contents

Table of Contents 3

A Note From History Compacted 5

Introduction 7

Chapter One: The Indian Problem 11

    The Land 15

Chapter Two: The Colonial Period 19

    King Philips War 23

    Pontiac's War 28

Chapter Three: Assimilation 33

    Tecumseh 36

    The Civilized Tribes 41

Chapter Four: Removal 44

    The Seminole Wars 46

    The Trail of Tears 49

Chapter Five: War 57

    Broken Promises 60

The Dakota War 61

Escalation of violence during the 1860s & 1870s 64

Red Cloud's War 66

Great Sioux War of 1876 68

Chapter Six: Massacre 75

The Ghost Dance 77

Wounded Knee 80

Chapter Seven: Kill the Indian, Save the Man 87

The Dawes Act 88

Boarding Schools 91

To the Present 95

Chapter Eight: The Noble Savage 100

Conclusion 105

References 111

About History Compacted 117

Dark Minds In History 119

A Note
From History Compacted

Hi there!

This is Jason Chen, founder of History Compacted. Before you continue your journey to the past, I want to take a quick moment to explain our position on history and the purpose of our books.

To us, history is more than just facts, dates, and names. We see history as pieces of stories that led to the world we know today. Besides, it makes it much more fun seeing it that way too.

That is why History Compacted was created: to tell amazing stories of the past and hopefully inspire you to search for more. After all, history would be too big for any one book. But what each book can give you is a piece of the puzzle to help you get to that fuller picture.

Lastly, I want to acknowledge the fact that history is often told from different perspectives. Depending on the topic and your upbringing, you might agree or disagree with how we present the facts. I understand disagreements are inevitable. That is why with a team of diverse writers, we aim to tell each story from a more neutral perspective. I hope this note can help you better understand our position and goals.

Now without further ado, let your journey to the past begins!

Introduction

"We hold these truths to be self-evident, that all men are created equal, that they are endowed by their Creator with certain unalienable Rights, that among these are Life, Liberty and the pursuit of Happiness."— US Declaration of Independence (1776)

When Thomas Jefferson wrote these words in 1776, he enshrined the lofty ideals and values that define American society.

America, he believed, would stand for self-government, individual rights, and above all, freedom. These ideals are woven in to the nation's DNA and are still a large part of the social and political fabric of the United States. However, this most-famous passage from the Declaration of Independence also preserves the uncomfortable and unavoidable reality that American history is full of contradictions.

Paradox is as strong and consistent of an American value as any of the lofty ideals that Jefferson and his fellow congressmen imagined. American history is full of examples where the "pursuit of happiness" for one requires the trampling on or destruction of another's life or liberty.

Many Americans prefer to focus on the remarkable determination and grit of American progress, while ignoring or minimizing the unpleasant acts it took to achieve that progress. Nowhere is this more evident in American history than the story of the United States relationship with Native Americans.

From the outset of the country, Native Americans were considered a problem. They were in the way of America's "manifest destiny." Americans saw the native "Indians" as a threat and impediment to the inevitable march of progress and civilization. To be clear, progress and civilization are not bad things. Americans were right in seeking to better their own society and their own lives.

However, the price that was paid for this "progress" was the genocide of an entire culture of Native Americans. This remains one of the darkest chapters in American history. For many Americans, this is a hard story to reconcile. Many prefer to sweep this chapter of American history under the rug and either pretend it did not happen or dismiss its severity.

How can a nation that has accomplished so much and prides itself on freedom and self-determination also be responsible for such genocide? For Americans, this is an understandably difficult contradiction to wrestle with.

So, enduring questions about this black mark on the American record remain. How did this happen? Why did it happen? Was it necessary or inevitable? Who is truly responsible? These are difficult, but important questions to consider. The answers that can be gathered are complicated, ugly, and have roots in belief systems that far pre-date the founding of United States.

"The Indian problem" was one that America struggled with from its outset, and in many ways is still struggling with, though the nature of the problem has changed dramatically over the centuries. The United States attempted many solutions to this "problem," and these solutions demonstrate both the best and worst of what America represents.

The story of the American Indian Wars is different from the average American war story. This is not a story of valor, heroism or glory. It is simply a tragedy.

Chapter One

The Indian Problem

Why did many Americans view the Indians as being "in the way," and a barrier to their success? Why did they view these native people as a problem that needed solving?

The easiest way to examine these questions is to go back to the beginning of this tortured relationship. The first sustained European contact with Native Americans occurred in 1492, when a small group of Spanish-funded explorers, led by Christopher Columbus, made landfall on a North American island in the Bahamas. Columbus and his men encountered the natives on this island, and made some interesting and telling observations.

In his diary from Thursday, October 11, 1492, Columbus wrote:

> *"But it seemed to me that they were a people very poor in everything. All of them go around as naked as their mothers bore them... They are very well formed, with handsome bodies and good faces. Their hair coarse -- almost like the tail of a horse... They do not carry arms nor are they acquainted with them, because I showed them swords and they took them by the edge and through ignorance cut themselves. They have no iron... They should be good and intelligent servants... and I believe that they would become Christians very easily, for it seemed to me that they had no religion. Our Lord pleasing, at the time of my departure I will take six of them from here to (Spain) in order that they may learn to speak."*

What is abundantly clear from Columbus's diary is that he immediately sees himself and his culture as being better than the natives. In a way, he believes the natives are sub-human, or at the very least, not *as* human as he and his European brethren. He discusses the native's bodies, hair, and form as if they were animals. He is astounded that the natives, not knowing what a sword was, grabbed a sword by the blade and cut themselves.

To any person in Europe, educated or not, this level of ignorance would be almost unthinkable, as Europeans had been fighting with swords for generations. Columbus sees these people as easy converts to Christianity and wants to teach some of them how to speak English. Columbus was the first of many to think that the natives should be "civilized," that is, to be made more like a European.

For Columbus, and so many that came after him, the driving force behind the treatment of Native Americans was the basic assumption that European civilization and culture were vastly superior to the native way of life. It is not hard to see why many Europeans, and later Americans, viewed their culture as better.

European/American culture had more advanced weapons and technology, settled agriculture that allowed for the creation of cities, and an organized and productive societal structure. Aside from major civilizations like the Aztecs, Native American communities largely did not have these features in their culture.

Natives were viewed as uncivilized and backwards savages that would be improved significantly if they adopted more "white" traditions. This ingrained belief of the natives being an inferior being is absolutely essential to understanding the attitude and action of the people and government of the United States toward the American Indians.

To go along with this ethno-centric belief system, Europeans also found religious justification for their actions. From the earliest days of Spanish colonization in North America, Native Americans were dying by the hundreds of thousands due to disease.

Europeans had brought old world germs and illnesses, like smallpox, plague, influenza, and measles—among many others—to the new world. The Native American immune system was completely unequipped to fight these new, deadly enemies. These diseases killed millions of natives and crippled their societies. Some historians estimate that as many as ninety percent of the Native American population was killed due to the influx of European disease.

This level of destruction on a group of people is almost unfathomable. To a European at the time, without a modern understanding of germs and medicine, this epidemic was largely interpreted as a sign from God that the Europeans were in the right.

Keep in mind; this was a time when religious zeal and piety was a much stronger force in the everyday life of the people and institutions of Europe. Christianity was used as a guiding principle for choices and behavior, but also as a justification for violence. Europeans felt tasked with spreading Christianity as the world's one true religion, and many believed that there was no greater cause than Christianity's triumph.

For Europeans during this period, it would have been an extremely logical conclusion that God would destroy non-Christian natives in favor of European colonizers, who often branded themselves as Christian warriors fighting to spread their faith to a new land. Europeans felt like they had God's approval to expand over the natives, which is absolutely critical in a time period where religion played such a large role in people's lives and decision making.

The Land

From the earliest days of the American colonial period, there was a distinct cultural divide between settlers and natives.

The ethnic, developmental, and religious differences between the groups were "baked in" to a relationship that was nearly always viewed from both sides as "us" versus "them." This divide only widened as America became more developed, yearned to grow, and occupied more land.

Native American tribes had lived on their land for generations, and their lifestyle was diverse and heavily dependent on their environment. Regardless of their tribal and environmental differences, the land was a harmonious part of Native American existence. Native Americans did not seek to tame or control the nature, but instead to live as one with the nature.

Many native tribes were more mobile, and used the land only as they needed it. As the Suquamish Chief Seattle said in 1854, "How can you buy or sell the sky, the warmth of the land? The idea is strange to us. If we do not own the freshness of the air and sparkle of the water, how can you buy them? We are part of the earth, and it is part of us."

Clearly, this attitude about land is incompatible with the American attitude. In 1802, John Quincy Adams, who would later become President, said, "Shall the fields and valleys, which a beneficent God has formed to teem with the life of innumerable multitudes, be condemned to everlasting barrenness?" Adams captured the American attitude about land perfectly.

Americans sought to own land and make that land productive for their own personal gain. To control and settle an area was a marker of progress. Land that was still untamed or not being used was considered a waste of a valuable resource. Americans would not stand idly by while valuable, profitable land was "condemned to everlasting barrenness." Simply put, Americans were always too ambitious to let the land be governed by Native American principles.

Natives were not turning the land into personal profit or being "productive," in the American sense of the word. There was too much money to be made, and too much progress to be had to let the Natives live as they had in pre-Columbian times. Native Americans could not and would not stand in the way of the inevitability of American progress.

This disagreement about the proper and rightful view of nature is a critical piece of context for understanding what happens later in this story. So much of the relationship between the U.S. and the Native Americans ultimately rests on these beliefs about land.

From the United States perspective, the land attitudes are more evidence of the native's cultural inferiority and backward ways. It also serves as the origin for the idea of the Indian reservation system that will come in the future.

From a Native American perspective, it is the first proof that the "white man" represents a permanent change in their situation, and a significant threat to their way of life. Native leaders would clearly recognize the severity of this threat, and for centuries they attempted to resist encroaching colonization and protect their people.

Chapter Two
The Colonial Period

During the earliest days of French and English settlement in North America, colonists and natives developed a mutually beneficial and peaceful relationship based on trade. Colonists in the early 17th Century were primarily interested in making money through the lucrative business of the fur trade.

Fur, especially deer hides and beaver pelts, were a valuable commodity because they could be made into high-demand clothing items to be sold in Europe. Success for fur-traders was heavily dependent on establishing friendly trading relationships with the Native American tribes they came in contact with. Fur-traders would give the natives iron tools, guns, blankets and cloth, in exchange for the desired furs—which the natives also had to hunt—and food for their own survival. This trade relationship helped and furthered both parties.

The colonists were making money, and the natives enjoyed the benefits of the new European technologies and goods that in many ways made their lives easier. This period of peace and cooperation began to fade as the number of colonists in North America continued to grow.

As settlements expanded, so did their ambition and need for more territory and resources. In the Virginia colony, the settlers of Jamestown and the local Powhatan tribe had a short-lived period of peace after the marriage of the Powhatan princess Pocahontas to the Englishmen John Rolfe.

Pocahontas is a good example of what the English hoped to achieve with their Powhatan neighbors. She converted to Christianity, took a Christian name; Rebecca, married an Englishman; Rolfe, and bore him a son, and in 1616, she left with her new family for London.

Pocahontas was considered to have been "civilized" by the colonists. This strategy of civilizing and Christianizing the Powhatan in order to envelop them into colonial society became even more crucial by 1620. The settlers of Jamestown were starting to realize the economic potential of the tobacco they were farming, and they needed to expand. The safest and easiest way for them grow was to create more "praying Indians"—natives who converted to Christianity—and live side by side with them.

This put the Powhatan in an almost impossible position. They were being asked to commit "cultural suicide," by casting all of their cultural traditions and beliefs aside in favor of joining the new European culture. Many natives did make this choice, but a great many others could not abandon their heritage so easily. This left with them with no other choice but to resist the new European culture, and resistance would mean violence.

In 1622, the Powhatan hatched a plan of attack they hoped would drive the colonists back to the sea, and expel them from North America once and for all. On the evening of March 21, 1622, the Powhatan arrived at the Jamestown settlement bearing gifts. They brought fruits, deer, turkey, and other foods to sell and share with the settlers. The next morning—March 22—as the settlers were beginning their work for the day, the Powhatan sprang into action.

They grabbed every tool or weapon they could find, and set to work slaughtering the English. Powhatan warriors bashed in English heads with hatchets, and shot any settlers who tried to flee. They went to the colonial plantations, killed the livestock, and burned the crops. The survivors, shocked at what was happening, retreated to the Jamestown fort for safety. When the dust settled, three hundred forty-seven English men, women, and children were dead. The death toll rose higher when winter came. The lack of livestock and crops caused many more settlers to die from starvation and illness.

From a Powhatan perspective, the raid was a success. However, they severely miscalculated what the English response would be. The Powhatan expected the English to acknowledge their defeat and sail back home. This assumption proved to be a grave error. The English stayed and licked their wounds at Jamestown, and with more ships from Europe arriving regularly, they regained their power and stability.

Jamestown had survived, and now the settlers had ample justification to be hostile toward their native neighbors. The English exacted their revenge on the Powhatan for the next decade. They raided and burned Powhatan villages, massacred their people, destroyed their crops, and seized their land. The colonists had asserted themselves as the masters of the area, and Powhatan power and influence in their ancestral homeland steadily declined until it was all but lost.

The Indian Massacre of 1622, though initially a success for the Powhatan, proved to be disastrous in the long-term due to the violent retribution that they faced in the years following the massacre. It was the beginning of the end of any semblance of life as the Powhatan knew it.

However, it is important to remember the predicament that the Powhatan were in. They were ultimately forced to choose their cultures fate; a slow death by assimilation, or a quicker but much more brutal death by violently resisting the colonists. The Powhatan tried, and failed, to save themselves and their culture from conquest by the Europeans. What else could they have done?

King Philips War

Native American tribes in New England would find themselves in very similar predicaments as the Powhatan in Jamestown, and ultimately would meet a similar fate.

New England was home to the Algonquin peoples, a series of independent tribes united by their similar language—Algonquin. When the radically Christian Puritans arrived in Plymouth in 1620, they relied on trade with the local Wampanoag tribe for survival. These early years of peace have been memorialized, if not highly romanticized, by the first Thanksgiving feast shared between the settlers and the natives, likely in 1621.

Despite the early cooperation and success of the fur trade, the Puritans viewed the Wampanoag and the other Algonquin tribes as vermin, in large part because of religious differences. Natives who converted to Christianity and became "praying Indians" were accepted, albeit as second class citizens.

Through the course of the 17th Century, tensions between the English and Native Americans rose as more settlers arrived, more native land was being taken, and more pressure to assimilate was being put on the natives.

For Metacom, the chief of the Wampanoag tribe—the English called him King Philip, it was clear to see that the current situation was untenable in the long-term. Metacom began planning a major attack he hoped would force the English to leave for good.

In January of 1675, John Sassamon, a "praying Indian" that had been educated at Harvard and served as an interpreter and advisor to Metacom, informed the Puritan leaders about Metacom's plan to attack. Sassamon subsequently disappeared during the winter. In early spring of 1675, Sassamon's body was found underneath the ice at a nearby pond, his neck broken.

The Puritans were outraged, and they accused three of Metacom's warriors for murdering Sassamon. The three warriors were found guilty and executed in June of 1675. The execution of these three native warriors lit the fuse of war between the Wampanoag and the English.

A band of Native Americans immediately rode to the small town of Swansea. The Natives laid siege, burned the town, and killed seven colonists. This prompted the colonial militia of Massachusetts Bay to mobilize for war. The year that followed was one of the bloodiest per-capita in American history, with terrible carnage levied by both sides against the other.

Metacom and his followers succeeded in burning and razing a dozen colonial towns, including Providence. They killed English settlers, destroyed English crops, and had much early success against the disorganized and poorly led colonial militia.

The English were equally brutal, massacring upwards of six hundred Naragansett—a tribe allied with the Wampanoag—men, women, and children at the Great Swamp Fight. It was not until English leaders capitalized on inter-tribal rivalries that they were able to turn the tide of the war in their favor. The English recruited Metacom's old native rivals to assist them in their war effort, which proved to be too great an obstacle to overcome for the Wampanoag. With his forces outnumbered and crippled by starvation and disease, Metacom was killed in August of 1676.

The English, seizing the opportunity to send a message, decapitated and quartered Metacom's corpse. They placed his head on a spike, and displayed it at the entrance to the city of Plymouth, where it remained for twenty-five years as a warning to rebellious minded natives.

King Philip's war was a struggle for both colonists and natives to attempt to preserve their way of life. Both sides suffered dearly for that cause. An estimated twenty-five hundred colonists were killed, which some believe was about thirty percent of the English population at the time.

For the natives, the outcome was even grimmer. Exact casualty numbers are unknown, but many believe that the number of natives killed was double that of the colonists. Aside from the incredibly high casualty rate, the war fundamentally changed the dynamic between natives and colonists in New England. The war drastically and permanently reduced the Algonquin power and influence in the region, and similarly to Jamestown, proved that the colonists would be the new masters of the land. It also established the future precedent for violence and war against Native Americans, especially for those natives who resisted assimilation.

King Philip's war was another failed Native American attempt to expel the English from their land and save their culture from being conquered. It is a cruel twist of fate that a huge factor in Metacom's ultimate undoing was the inability of the native tribes to unify and fight against their common enemy. Many native tribes believed it best to befriend and militarily ally with the colonists as a way to gain dominance over rival native tribes, and achieve peace with their new European neighbors.

This strategy may have garnered short-term benefits for individual tribes, but the Native American inability to unify and act with a common purpose made it all the easier for the English to "divide and conquer" the native peoples. Had those tribes, who allied with the English against Metacom backed their native brethren instead, the outcome of King Philip's war may have turned out differently.

Pontiac's War

For the rest of the 17th and well in to mid-18th century, natives and colonists saw a continuation of both fur-trading alliances and rising tension between their groups. As both British and French fur trading operations grew, so did the value of the land in the Ohio River valley.

This land was prime real estate for the profitable expansion of the fur trade, and both the British and French made competing claims for the land. These land disputes ultimately led to war between Britain and France in North America, and both countries employed loyal Native American tribes to fight for their respective sides.

The British ultimately won the so-called "French and Indian war," which had several lasting implications. One of the most significant impacts of the war was re-drawing of the territorial map of North America. France had been defeated, and thus, ceded their colonies and land claims in North America to the British in 1763. The British now had control over former French lands, and the British leadership was not well received by their new Native American subjects.

The Native Americans living the Ohio Valley felt threatened by their new British overlords. The local British government restricted trade with the natives and interfered with their ability to hunt. In response to the fears of encroaching British power, the Odawa leader named Pontiac rallied together warriors from several area tribes and went about attacking British forts, hoping to expel the British from their lands. Pontiac's rebellion further escalated the tradition of downright brutal fighting between the natives and the British.

Throughout the summer and fall of 1763, Pontiac and his men viciously captured and destroyed eight of the eleven British forts in the area. Pontiac and his men committed atrocities that absolutely terrified the settlers in the area. The natives scalped their vanquished enemies, tortured survivors, killed surrendering soldiers, and even engaged in ritual cannibalization.

Amidst the bloodshed of war, British civilian casualties ended up being higher than the military casualties. Pontiac, while successful in a military sense, had intensified the conflict between natives and colonists to a more radical and violent state.

The British fought back against Pontiac in different, but equally brutal ways. While Pontiac was sieging the British stronghold at Fort Pitt, British leadership devised a plan to use biological warfare against the natives. The British proceeded to infect a number of blankets with smallpox, and when they received Native American envoys into the fort to discuss peace, gave the infected blankets to the natives in the hopes it would spread the deadly disease through their camp.

Historian's debate about the effectiveness of the smallpox blankets in killing natives, but the use of biological warfare represents a larger point about the nature of this conflict. Biological weapons are designed for indiscriminate mass killings. They are not normal weapons of war. They are weapons of genocide. This new policy, along with Pontiac's terrorism in the Ohio Valley, denotes an unpleasant new low in Native American and British relations. Pontiac's war was becoming a war of extermination.

The British were able to regroup in 1764, and stop any further progress of Pontiac's forces. In 1766, with the two sides basically at stalemate, a peace treaty was reached that incorporated new land laws from the Royal Proclamation of 1763. This proclamation, which had been passed shortly after the rebellion began, was three years old at this point, and forbade any colonial settlement in land west of the Appalachians.

That land, which had been acquired from the French, was to be set aside for the Native Americans. The proclamation even refers to the territory as an Indian reservation. The British government in London saw this reservation as an alternative solution to the vicious cycle that had been repeating itself since Jamestown. In theory, moving the natives to the reservation would appease them because they would be far away from colonial encroachment. It would also protect the colonists from Native American attacks and clear the way for continued development in the already established colonies.

The issue with the Proclamation of 1763 was that it did not work in reality as it had in theory. Colonists basically ignored it, and settled in the new western territory anyway. The people of the colonies could see that some day, in the not too distant future, that land would be incredibly valuable. This is one of the first examples of the colonists outright rejecting a decision made by the British crown.

The Proclamation of 1763 made colonists realize that the King might not always be right in matters regarding governance of their homes halfway across the world in North America. Perhaps they, the people of the colonies, knew better. For the colonists, the road to revolution had begun. For the natives, they were dealing with a familiar problem. The British settlers were again encroaching on their land. Unfortunately for the Native Americans, this would be a pattern that continued throughout the 19th century.

Chapter Three
Assimilation

Native Americans continued living on the frontier which had been "reserved" for them, and they remained in a state of violent resistance against American expansion on their lands.

The last quarter of the 18th century saw nearly continuous violence between Americans and Native Americans somewhere on the frontier. Exacerbating the problem was the legacy of brutality and distrust leftover from the colonial period.

The newly born United States remembered the atrocities committed by Pontiac and Metacom, which made it easy for them frame the natives as barbaric savages. At the same time, the Native Americans remembered the massive cultural destruction that "the white man" had caused, and now they were witnessing U.S. settlers breaking their agreement of an undisturbed Indian reservation. Both sides were scared of the other, and both were more than willing to use violence to gain the upper hand.

This status-quo changed dramatically in 1803, when President Thomas Jefferson orchestrated what many claim to be the best real-estate deal in history. The Louisiana Purchase more than doubled the size of the United States, opening up a massive new frontier to the west. Settling and expanding westward was a tremendous opportunity for the United States, but once again, the "Indian problem" posed some difficult questions for the U.S. government.

What should be done about all of the new tribes that now lived in the United States? How could the U.S. expand west on to native land in the safest way possible? Could the natives be pushed even further west, to the edge of the new territory, in order to clear space for American development?

These questions, among many others, were on Jefferson's mind when he commissioned Meriwether Lewis and William Clark to explore the new Louisiana territory. He told Lewis and Clark to be as friendly as possible with the natives they encountered on their journey. He also asked them to gather all sorts of information about the native tribes so that "it may better enable those who may endeavor to civilize & instruct them."

Lewis and Clark followed Jefferson's orders. They famously relied on the navigation instructions from the Shoshone interpreter Sacagawea, who greatly assisted Lewis and Clark in their journey to the Pacific Ocean.

More importantly, Jefferson's instructions to Lewis and Clark showed that he wanted to take the sensible and non-violent approach of "civilizing" the natives. From the American perspective, this approach was kind, benevolent, and much easier for everyone. Most Americans at the time wholeheartedly believed that their culture was better than the natives, which meant that natives could "improve themselves" and be peaceful neighbors with Americans if they adopted American culture and learned to farm.

Americans saw the easiest and most peaceful solution to the Indian problem as giving the "savages" the gift of Christianity and civilization. Clearly this perspective is ethno-centric and completely ignores the value of Native

American culture, which is ultimately why this strategy would never work on a large scale.

While Jefferson's strategy had some success in certain areas, this new period of American expansion turned out to just be more of the same pattern that had been established during colonial times.

Tecumseh

The latest iteration of this similar pattern occurred on the frontier of the new Indiana territory. The land that contains present day Ohio, Indiana, and Illinois was a major area of focus for U.S. expansion because the land was rich in natural resources. Indiana officially became an organized U.S. territory in 1800, and appointed its first governor, William Henry Harrison, in 1801.

As the Americans scouted, surveyed, and settled this new land, the natives once again felt threatened by American encroachment. This time, however, the Native American resistance to American expansion was more formidable.

Tecumseh, chief of the local Shawnee tribe, learned from the mistakes of Metacom. He organized a massive confederation of Indian tribes united by the common purpose of defending their land and their way of life. As Tecumseh himself put it, "A single twig breaks, but a bundle of twigs is strong." This Indian Confederacy was a strong alliance and realistically was the best strategy for the Native Americans to take. However, Tecumseh's "bundle of twigs" was not as tightly wound as he had thought.

In 1809, a group of Native American leaders—NOT acting under the orders of Tecumseh—met with Governor Harrison to discuss selling their land. Harrison was delighted and more than willing to pay for the peaceful expansion of his territory. A deal was struck, and Harrison and his men immediately went to work "settling" the land. However, a deal of this nature runs counter to the Native American belief in collective land use, a belief that Tecumseh still very much subscribed to. When he heard of the deal that ceded over three million acres of native land to the Americans, he was furious, and thought of the treaty as illegitimate.

In his rage, Tecumseh gathered a band of four hundred warriors, fully armed, painted for war, and marched to Governor Harrison's house. He "met" with Harrison and demanded that the treaty be rescinded. Harrison, being a proper and "civilized" man, told Tecumseh that the deal was perfectly legal because the land belonged to the chiefs, whom he had bought it from. To this, Tecumseh retorted:

"Sell a country! Why not sell the air, the great sea, as well as the earth? Did not the Great Spirit make them all for the use of his children? How can we have confidence in the white people?"

Tecumseh's warriors began to draw their weapons, and some witnesses believe that Tecumseh was ordering them to kill the Governor. With the situation dangerously escalating, Harrison himself drew his sword, and his officers and security detail drew their firearms, preparing for an attack. Fortunately, some of Tecumseh's aides talked him down and convinced Tecumseh and the warriors to leave peacefully. Bloodshed had been narrowly avoided.

The bloodshed that was avoided that day in 1810, was merely postponed until November of 1811. Harrison rightfully felt threatened by Tecumseh and wanted to eliminate the barrier to American expansion on his new land. When Tecumseh was away traveling to recruit other tribes to join him, Harrison led the Indiana militia to attack Tecumseh's home and his men situated on the Tippecanoe River.

After withstanding a ferocious assault from the natives, Harrison and the Americans drove the natives off their land and burned their settlement to the ground. Harrison's victory at the Battle of Tippecanoe removed the threat of Tecumseh from his land. However, Tecumseh was not finished with his violent resistance to American expansion.

Tecumseh and what was left of his confederacy fled to Canada, where they allied with the British and fought on their side during the War of 1812. For Tecumseh, the alliance with Britain was the last hope of truly stopping the American conquest of the continent and establishing a Native American homeland.

Tecumseh and his warriors were instrumental in the siege and British capture of Fort Detroit in August of 1812. When the U.S., attempting to regain Fort Detroit, was stopped at Frenchtown in January of 1813, Tecumseh was once again in the spotlight.

Tecumseh, not wanting to accommodate U.S. prisoners of war, decided to execute them. He set the hospital on fire, leaving the wounded inside to either burn alive, or if they were able to escape the flames, to have their heads split open by a Shawnee tomahawk. Tecumseh killed between thirty and one hundred U.S. Prisoners of war at the River Raisin Massacre.

Tecumseh continued commanding his warriors alongside the British through most of 1813. In October of 1813, Tecumseh was killed during an American attack on the Thames.

While it is unclear how he died, most historians believe that American troops mutilated his body after he was killed as a way to exact revenge for the River Raisin Massacre.

With Tecumseh dead, the Indian confederation fell apart. The war ended in 1815, without a clear winner, and the only true loser being the Native Americans. The War of 1812 cemented the inevitability of the American domination of the continent, which would leave the natives crushed under the heel of American "manifest destiny."

Tecumseh, despite trying new and frankly better strategies than his predecessors like Metacom and Pontiac, ultimately met the same fate. He made the choice to fight for the preservation of his culture and home, and gave his life for that end.

Tecumseh is a legendary figure in American history, and many Americans even admire his zeal and dedication to his cause. However, this was not enough to achieve his ultimate goal, and the Native Americans would never again really threaten to impede U.S. expansion in the west. The dream of a large sovereign nation of Indians died with Tecumseh.

The Civilized Tribes

Tribes in the south adopted a different strategy than Tecumseh: partial assimilation. For people in the Cherokee, Chickasaw, Choctaw, Muskogee, and Seminole tribes, the best way to preserve anything resembling their culture was to play by the new, American rules.

They believed—based on what they were told by Thomas Jefferson—that if they could assimilate enough into American culture and fit American values, they would be able to keep their land and thus, preserve at least a part of their unique identity.

These tribes became settled on their land, began practicing modern settled agricultural techniques, and became active participants in the U.S. economy. These tribes developed more centralized and formal government structures, often with written constitutions, and had official diplomatic relations with the United States.

They integrated education and literacy into their cultures, learned to speak English, and some even developed the first writing systems for their own ancient, spoken native languages. In short, they were leading lives very similar to many Americans. Like many other Native American self-preservation strategies, this was effective for a short time.

Americans were happy to have peaceful relations with the natives provided they were not in the way of American progress. However, when the U.S. decided they wanted the land the Indians resided on, it was all too easy for them to forget about agreements and peace and look to expel the natives from their land.

On the frontier, it was at least arguable to an American settler that stepping on Native American freedom was justified because of atrocities committed by people like Tecumseh. This same line of thinking would be completely invalid if applied to the treatment of the Five Civilized Tribes in the south.

These tribes were, in essence, doing exactly what the U.S. government of Jefferson hoped that all natives would do. They were becoming more "white." and started to fit into the culture of the United States. However, despite what could be construed as "progress" toward the goal of assimilating Indians, the presence of these tribes in their home land ultimately led to an American policy that is difficult to justify and still a major black eye for the country.

Chapter Four

Removal

In 1828, the United States elected a new President that dramatically changed the course of American politics. Andrew Jackson, a Tennessee democrat, a war hero, a national celebrity and "the man of the people," took office and fundamentally changed the United States.

His views on Native Americans differed from the presidents of the Jeffersonian era. Jefferson and his successors sought assimilation first, and had allowed "civilized" tribes like the Seminole and Cherokee to stay on their lands east of the Mississippi river as long as they adopted American cultural practices.

Jackson saw things differently. He wanted all the land east of the Mississippi River to be American. He wanted the natives sent to reservations in far off western territories, which in Jackson's time were new and still largely unsettled. His solution to the "Indian problem" was one of his primary campaign issues and he had been leading the charge for a policy of Indian removal for years. Once he got to the White House, he wasted little time in pursuing this policy.

Jackson began work with his southern brethren in Congress to make his campaign ideas about Indian removal into a reality. The issue sharply fell along party and sectional lines, as Jackson was an extremely polarizing force in this era of American politics. Indian removal was extremely popular in the South, especially to states that had a vested interest in removing one of the civilized tribes that resided on "their" land.

The Southern slave economy only stood to gain from the land and natural resources they could acquire. Opponents of the Indian Removal bill—and opponents of Jackson generally—argued against the idea of American imperialism, but in reality were arguing against the possible expansion of economic and political power that the South stood to gain from this land acquisition. The bill narrowly passed the House and the Senate with the necessary majority, and in 1830, President Jackson signed into federal law the *Indian Removal Act.*

The *Indian Removal Act* gave the President power to give natives a piece of unsettled land in the western territories—in present day Oklahoma—in exchange for their land east of the Mississippi river.

Jackson was confident that he could use his power to manipulate or pressure the Five Civilized Tribes to leaving their homes and relocating onto their new, "permanent" reservations. Jackson proved to be correct in his estimation.

The relationship between the Native Americans and the United States had changed once again. The U.S. sought a new solution to the age old "Indian problem." The era of Indian removal had begun.

The Seminole Wars

As one might expect, the Native American tribes largely did not take too kindly to the policy of forced removal. Each tribe reacted a bit differently, but the most violent resistance to the Indian Removal Act was from the Seminole tribe of

Florida, who were not keen on leaving their ancestral homeland

In 1832, a group of Seminoles, not necessarily representing the interests of everyone, traveled west to inspect a proposed new Seminole reservation at the behest of the U.S. government. If they found the land suitable, they would sign a treaty and officially cede their land in Florida to the United States, and the Seminole would move to the reservation.

These Seminole delegates decided the land was suitable and signed the treaty, which was ratified by the U.S. Congress in 1834. According to the Indian Removal Act, the land deal was official. The U.S. gave the Seminole until the end of 1835 to move off their land.

Many Seminole left peacefully, but a vast majority did not. Much of the Seminole leadership did not recognize the treaty as legitimate because they did not personally agree to its terms. They did not view the U.S. claims to Seminole land as being legitimate, and refused to leave.

The U.S. sent troops to nearby Fort King, hoping that a U.S. military presence would threaten the Seminoles enough to nudge them out. This was a miscalculation by the United

States. On December 28, 1835, the Seminoles, led by Chief Osceola, brutally shot and scalped Wiley Thompson, a former U.S. Congressman from Georgia, who was there as a negotiator for the U.S. government.

At the same time, a group of one hundred eighty Seminole warriors ambushed an unsuspecting and unprepared group of American soldiers near Fort King. The Seminoles achieved such surprise and deadly efficiency during this attack that the U.S. troops could never organize their defenses and fight back. One hundred and seven—out of one hundred and ten—American troops were killed in what is now called the Dade massacre.

The bloodshed on December 28th kickstarted the American war machine. Money and troops were raised to go to Florida and fight the rebellious Seminoles. The war dragged on for nearly seven years, as the Seminoles fiercely resisted, but were gradually overwhelmed by the size and force of the American military.

Thousands of Seminoles died in battle, and even more from disease and starvation. Thousands more were relocated, both forcibly and voluntarily, to their new reservation in Oklahoma. By the end of the war in 1842, there were fewer than one hundred Seminole warriors remaining in Florida.

The Seminole tribe had resisted, and just like their predecessors, were beaten and virtually wiped out. The Seminole certainly made it difficult for the American policy of Indian removal to be effective, but in the end, the Seminole were no longer a large presence in Florida, and the way was clear for American expansion on to that land. Though costly, Jackson's Indian removal in Florida was a success.

The Trail of Tears

Less violent approaches were taken by other tribes, but a peaceful approach would not save them from the unimaginable brutality they would experience during forced removal. The best example of this new approach is the way the Cherokee tribe went about resisting the Indian Removal Act.

In 1830, the state of Georgia, who had long coveted the Cherokee land, started making state laws that infringed on the sovereignty of the Cherokee. The Cherokee responded to this new law in an ironically classic American way: they took the Government to court.

The Cherokee claimed the state of Georgia had no legal right to take their land. In 1831, *Cherokee Nation vs Georgia* made it to the Supreme Court. The court ultimately threw the case out because they did not recognize the Cherokee as an independent, sovereign nation.

Chief Justice John Marshall classified the Cherokee as a "dependent nation," which was a new and unclear kind of classification. The Cherokee were not independent, nor were they Americans, nor were they conquered people—through the eyes of U.S. law. A "dependent nation," almost like a child is a dependent on their parents until they come of age. This is a strange and historically unique distinction, but one that would be clarified soon.

The following year, the Cherokee were back in court to defend their legal jurisdiction over the land. The 1832 case or *Worcester vs Georgia* was much more favorable for the Cherokee. The U.S. Supreme Court ruled that the state of Georgia had no legal right or jurisdiction to make laws over Indian held land. Amazingly, the Cherokee had won.

The Cherokee had opted for a non-violent, legal battle instead of violent resistance like the Seminole. For the time being, they were successful. The Cherokee were forging a new path of Indian resistance to American encroachment; beat the Americans at their own game.

How could the Americans justify breaking their own laws and removing a people that had proven to be just as "civilized" as them? As John Howard Payne, a writer who lived with the Cherokee for a time wrote:

> "When the Georgian asks, shall savages infest our borders thus? The Cherokee answers him, do we not read? Have we not schools? Churches? Manufacturers? Have we not laws? Letters? A constitution? And do you call us savages?"

This Cherokee success was rather short-lived. After the ruling, President Jackson supposedly—and likely, mythically—said, "(Supreme Court Chief Justice) John Marshall has made his decision; now, let him enforce it." Jackson had lost the battle, but was determined to use his power to win the war against the Cherokee.

After the unfavorable court decision, Jackson negotiated an extremely questionable treaty with an unelected Cherokee delegate who did not represent the opinion of the majority of the Cherokee people or their leadership. This delegate agreed to a treaty that sold the Cherokee land in Georgia to the U.S. in exchange for land on the reservation in Oklahoma.

This was a fatal blow to the tribe, because it gave the U.S. the power to remove them under the new Indian Removal Act. Similarly to the Seminoles, the two sides had "agreed" on a treaty in compliance with the new law, which meant the U.S. now "owned" the Cherokee land.

Cherokee leadership refused to accept the treaty as being legitimate and would not leave. This meant it was time for Jackson—and his successor Martin Van Buren, who was as Jacksonian as they come—to "enforce it," as he had promised that he would.

Years earlier, Supreme Court Justice John Marshall had temporarily saved the Cherokee with his pen. Andrew Jackson, staying true to his word and armed with both the law and an army, proved that in the case of Indian removal, the sword was indeed mightier than the pen.

In 1838, the United States sent seven thousand troops to Georgia to forcibly, at gunpoint, drag the Cherokee from their homes and remove them from their land. The U.S. military was now in charge of overseeing around fifteen thousand Cherokee men, women, and children relocate from Georgia to their new homes in Oklahoma.

The journey that fifteen thousand Cherokee were about to embark on was over eight hundred miles. If they were fortunate, they loaded everything they could carry on a wagon, or rode their horses. Many Cherokee, however, would be forced to walk. To make matters more difficult, most had no shoes or at best, shoes that were not designed for a thousand mile walk through rough terrain. Additionally, they were leaving late in the fall without proper clothing or supplies for the upcoming winter weather.

This forced march was a tragedy waiting to happen. Even the American commanding General Winfield Scott, whose nickname was "Old fuss and feathers," implored the Cherokee to move peacefully. He told them, "I am an old warrior, and have been present at many a scene of slaughter. But spare me; I beseech you, the horror of witnessing the destruction of the Cherokees." Unfortunately, General Scott would not get his wish.

Over the course of the four month journey, approximately four thousand Cherokee died on what is now called the, "Trail of Tears." They mostly died from exposure to the freezing temperatures, disease, malnutrition, and exhaustion. Private John Burnett, an American soldier, who was one of the "enforcers" said:

> "...the sufferings of the Cherokee were awful. The trail of exiles was a trail of death. They had to sleep in the wagons and on the ground without fire. And I have known as many as twenty-two of them to die in one night of pneumonia due to ill treatment, cold and exposure. Among this number was the beautiful Christian wife of Chief John Ross. This noble hearted woman died... giving her only blanket for the protection of a sick child. She rode... through a blinding sleet and snow storm, developed pneumonia and died in the still hours of a bleak winter night."

In addition to the massive Cherokee suffering, the Choctaw, Chickasaw, and Creek tribes had their own trails of tears. Forced removals left thirty-five hundred Creek dead—out of nearly twenty thousand who were being relocated, between three thousand and five thousand Choctaw dead—out of around seventeen thousand being relocated and around five hundred Chickasaw—out of around four thousand relocated.

In all, the Indian Removal Act and subsequent removal methods likely killed somewhere between ten thousand and fifteen thousand Native Americans. The U.S. forcibly removed and relocated almost fifty thousand more natives.

These Indian survivors forged on in their new Oklahoma reservation but were without around one third of their population. Extinguishing such a huge percentage of their respective tribes, in addition to separating each tribe from their ancestral homelands, represented a loss in tradition and values that the natives would never be able to fully recoup. This was another devastating loss of both life and culture for the Native Americans.

The butchery and cruelty shown during the Indian Removal Act is among the most shameful chapters in American history. This is one of the first examples—but nowhere near the last—of the United States, a country that proclaims the values of self-government and individual liberties, acting in a cold-blooded, imperialistic manner.

It is impossible to blame any single American or specific group of Americans for the Trail of Tears. This death march was the product of the over three hundred year old toxic relationship between the natives and the "white man." The Trail of Tears was the sum of all the past atrocities, violence, and American ethno-centric beliefs that had begun the moment that Columbus set foot on North American soil.

Americans truly believed themselves to be more human than the natives. This kind of categorization of people, where one is human and one is not, is an absolutely necessary ingredient to genocide. The Trail of Tears is an unmistakable marker of a genocide being practiced by the United States against the Native Americans. It is an outcome of hundreds of years of festering ethno-centrism and social Darwinism, and it forever fractured the relationship between Native Americans and the United States.

Chapter Five
War

One essential component for the success of the Indian Removal Act was the idea of the Indian reservation. These were promised and permanent Indian settlements in the west, where Indians would be far away from interfering with American progress or threatening American lives.

These lands were officially given to the Indians from the United States government in accordance with United States law. Like many other ideas and solutions presented by the Americans, this system worked well while it was politically expedient. The moment that American interests shifted or expanded in a manner that made those treaties no longer expedient, the United States found a way to stack the deck, once again, in their favor.

The history of the Indian reservation system is wrought with broken promises, bad deals, and the trampling over Native American natural rights by the United States of America.

The first shift in the expediency of the reservation system was the discovery of gold in the new California territory in 1848. Thousands of Americans crossed the continent in the hope of striking it rich in California, and they had to go through the Indian lands in order to get there. Once again, the Indians were "in the way."

Americans migrating westward inevitably meant settlement along the trail to some extent, which again meant encroaching on Indian Territory. This was a dangerous endeavor by Americans for many reasons, one of which was the threat of being attacked by Native Americans, hoping to drive them off their lands.

Geronimo, the famous Apache chief, led bands of warriors on raids in the west for nearly thirty years. He and his men would steal food, equipment, livestock, and kill Americans that he had stolen from. This kind of resistance was a threat to individual Americans, but was more of an annoyance to the big picture of American expansion.

The United States had their sights set on the building of a trans-continental railroad. This would not only keep travelers safe from Native American raids, it would also speed up the travel considerably. Faster travel meant more, and easier, connections between the two coasts, which would foster increased trade and new markets for goods.

The railroad represented an opportunity for massive wealth and huge economic gain, and the U.S. recognized that the Indian reservations were a barrier that would have to be cleared before such a railroad could exist.

Stephen Douglas, the famous Illinois Senator who was a huge proponent of the trans-continental railroad and a huge opponent of the Indian reservation, said:

"The idea of arresting our progress in that direction has become so ludicrous that we are amazed, that wise and patriotic statesman ever cherished the thought... How are we to develop, cherish and protect our immense interests and possessions on the Pacific, with a vast wilderness fifteen hundred miles in breadth, filled with hostile savages, and cutting off all direct communication? The Indian barrier must be removed."

In just one decade since the Cherokee suffering on the Trail of Tears, the permanent reservations that were legally given to the natives were starting to look awfully inconvenient for the United States.

Broken Promises

In 1851, the United States negotiated a treaty with a group of tribes at Fort Laramie, Wyoming. This treaty allowed Americans some limited access to Indian lands, in exchange for annual payments to the tribes and U.S. military protection. The treaty started to break down in 1854, when a small dispute over a cow turned in to the murder of a Sioux chief.

The Sioux responded by attacking and massacring thirty-one American troops, in what is now called the Grattan Massacre. This was the first battle in a war between the U.S. and the Sioux that would last thirty-seven years.

One year later, the United States would have their revenge for the Grattan Massacre. At Ash Hollow, the U.S. army attacked and overwhelmed a Sioux village, killing eighty-six and capturing seventy Sioux men, women, and children.

To fight a war against the United States, the Sioux were badly outnumbered and outgunned to begin with, so their chances at victory in an all-out war were slim at best. Fortunately for the Sioux, the attention of the United States was diverted elsewhere. The U.S. was spiraling into civil war based on the dispute over slavery.

Much of that dispute regarded the settlement of the western territories, and whether those new territories would be free, or slave-holding. The Civil War did not end the violence between the U.S. and Native Americans, but it was an interruption that slowed down the pace of the conflict.

The Dakota War

Most of the fighting in the American Civil War took place east of the Mississippi river, but there were natives involved in the "trans-Mississippi" theater of the war. Natives fought for both the Union and the Confederacy, but were not a significant factor in the outcome of the war. Most natives were content with being left alone on their reservations, far away from the bloodshed that engulfed the United States from 1861-1865.

However, just because many were not fighting, does not mean that they were untouched by the effects of war. The

U.S. government focused all of its attention and resources in fighting the Confederacy, and that meant they often did not pay or were very late on their agreed upon annual land payments to Native Americans. The breakdown of treaty payments caused a violent uprising in Minnesota in 1862.

The Dakota Sioux in Minnesota were heavily reliant on payments from the U.S. government in order to have enough food to survive. By the summer of 1862, the situation was growing desperate. Due to the encroachment of settlers, the population of bison and other game had reduced and the Dakota could not sustain themselves through hunting, and land was not fertile enough to sustain them through farming. When those treaty payments stopped coming in, they could not pay traders and merchants for their food supplies.

This desperation exploded in to war in August of 1862, when a small group of Dakota hunters killed five American settlers and stole their goods. The Dakota chief, Little Crow, decided to turn this skirmish into the start of an all-out offensive. For the next month, a band of Dakota warriors attacked white settlements in Minnesota with the hope of driving the Americans out of their land forever. They destroyed American settlements, attacked stagecoaches passing through the territory, killed hundreds of American civilians, and caused hundreds more to flee for their lives.

President Lincoln finally had to divert troops from the Civil War to go to Minnesota and put down this rebellion, which they did fairly quickly. By the end of September, the U.S. army had defeated the Dakota and taken thousands of them as prisoners.

In their thirst for revenge, the U.S. military tribunals tried four hundred and ninety-eight Dakota for war crimes. Three hundred and three were found guilty and sentenced to death. These trials were mostly a show, as the natives were not given defense attorneys and some trials were finished in less than five minutes. Ultimately, President Lincoln commuted the death sentence of all but thirty-eight of the convicted Dakota.

On December 26, 1862, thirty-eight Dakota were hanged in Mankato, Minnesota. This is still the largest mass execution in American history, and it could have been significantly worse if not for the last minute mercy shown by Lincoln.

The Dakota war is a symbol of the new type of relationship that existed between the natives and the

Americans during this period. Natives found themselves in a very unusual conundrum. They had virtually no bargaining power. They were almost completely reliant on the United States for survival, yet at the same time, they recognized that the U.S. military could crush them in an instant if they stood up for themselves.

For centuries, Native Americans had tried to secure a peaceful future. War had failed them time and time again. Peace and negotiation had failed them time and time again. What else could the natives realistically do? Their worst fears were being realized.

Escalation of violence during the 1860s & 1870s

The aftermath of the Dakota war once again damaged the relationship and trust between settlers and Native Americans. This distrust exploded into more violence in Colorado in 1863.

The 1851 Treaty of Fort Laramie had been renegotiated in 1861, with very favorable terms for the United States. Many local Cheyenne Indians were unhappy with the redrawing of the new reservation boundaries, and simply ignored them. They continued to hunt and live where they wanted, even though they were not on their legal reservation.

With the U.S. army more occupied with Confederate troops than the Cheyenne, there was no initial resistance to the Cheyenne breaking the law.

By 1864, with the Confederate threat in Colorado gone, attention was now solely focused on the Cheyenne. The army was under the command of Colonel John Chivington, who was extremely hostile to the Native Americans. He, along with the Colorado territorial government, viewed the Cheyenne as a huge threat to their safety. Chivington said:

> *"Damn any man who sympathizes with Indians! ...I have come to kill Indians, and believe it is right and honorable to use any means under God's heaven to kill Indians. ...Kill and scalp all, big and little; nits make lice."*

Chivington made good on his brutal promise. In November of 1864, Chivington led his men to a peaceful Native American encampment at Sand Creek, where they proceeded to slaughter everyone inside. Around one hundred thirty natives were killed, with over one hundred of those being women or children.

Chivington and his men scalped their victims, mutilated their bodies, and took body parts as trophies in to town to display at the local saloons. The Cheyenne retaliated in the months that followed by attacking the stagecoach station and some local ranches. Being vastly outnumbered, however, the Cheyenne moved north in to the Black Hills, in the hope of avoiding violence and hostility they had seen from the Americans in Colorado. Unfortunately for them, that hope would not be realized.

Once again, Americans had broken treaties and escalated violence with the plains Indians. This pattern had been occurring for years, and each time it benefited Americans at the expense of the natives. The pattern was brutally effective, which is why the Americans continued to utilize it, despite the dishonor that comes with breaking an agreement. For the United States, the wars on the plains were just another example of the ends justifying the means, whatever those means might be.

Red Cloud's War

The legacy of violence and infringement on promised Native American land seen in Minnesota and Colorado was major concern for all remaining Native American tribes. The Americans were not respecting their boundaries, and natives were left with very little that they could do in response.

In 1866, Americans once again violated Indian land when they started building forts along the Bozeman trail, which ran right through Lakota Sioux territory in present day Wyoming and Montana. The Lakota Sioux chief, Red Cloud, was committed to learning from the mistakes of his brethren in Minnesota in 1862, and wanted to stop American encroachment on his land before it became too late.

Red Cloud devised a brilliant and fairly modern strategy. He would not directly attack the forts themselves, but rather the wagon trains going to supply and fortify the forts.

The wagon trains were not as well defended, and they were out in the open, where he believed he had the advantage over fighting the Americans when they were fortified. If successful, he could also starve out American supplies and make it difficult for them to continue to fight and live on his people's land.

This worked incredibly well, as he routed the Americans during the Fetterman fight in late 1866. He continued winning great victories through 1867.

By 1868, the Americans were ready to negotiate a peace with Red Cloud to end the string of defeats they had endured.

The second treaty of Fort Laramie in 1868 established a Great Sioux reservation that stretched from parts of Montana through South Dakota, Wyoming, and Nebraska.

Red Cloud had won. He expelled the Americans from his land, and secured a permanent reservation for his people. Not only that, but he secured this land through success on the battlefield. This is one of the very few examples where the Native Americans were negotiating from a position of strength over the Americans.

Red Cloud had done, temporarily, what so many native leaders before him had failed to do. He had beaten the Americans. He out-strategized them and won a great peace for his people. However, Red Cloud recognized that no strategy, no matter how brilliant, could overcome the overwhelming force of people and technology the Americans represented. He had won the battle, but Red Cloud knew that negotiation was the key for his people not to completely lose the war that was to come.

Great Sioux War of 1876

Red Cloud's great victory and establishment of peace would only last for six years. By 1874, Americans had discovered gold in the Black Hills, part of the Great Sioux Reservation.

Americans began illegally mining on native land. The U.S. Army, beholden to the treaty and not wanting more violence, tried to keep U.S. settlers off of Sioux land. However, American settlers, prospecting for more gold, continued to cross the borders illegally to mine.

This was unacceptable to the powerful local chiefs Crazy Horse and Sitting Bull. They beseeched the American government to stop the flow of miners in to their land. However, with the prospect of gold and the value of the natural resources found in the Black Hills, American interests and policy had shifted. The treaty, which had been signed six years prior, was no longer politically expedient. The Americans wanted that land.

In 1874, the United States sent a cavalry unit, led by Civil War hero George Armstrong Custer, to the Black Hills to explore the territory and establish a U.S. fort in the region. This greatly alarmed the Native Americans, as they rightfully were concerned about history repeating itself in some form.

In 1875, a delegation of Sioux leaders, led by Red Cloud, went to Washington, DC, to meet with President

Ulysses S. Grant, hoping Grant would reaffirm the treaty and respect their reservation.

Grant and the U.S. government offered to buy the land from the Sioux, and relocate the Sioux to the Oklahoma reservation. Of course, these were unacceptable terms for the Native Americans, who insisted on staying on their land. The two sides were at an impasse. Americans wanted to buy the land, but the land was not for sale by its legal owner, the Sioux.

With pressure mounting on Grant that the Black Hills be somehow taken by the U.S., the government issued an ultimatum to the Sioux. They insisted that all of the "off-reservation" Indians in the Black Hills, who were under the command of Sitting Bull, be back on the reservation no later than January 31, 1876.

This ultimatum was a U.S. strategy for justifying war with the Sioux. They knew it would be difficult to get word to any "off reservation" Indians in time for the deadline. The U.S. needed an excuse to attack, and formulated a nearly impossible ultimatum in order to gain that justification. The U.S. had successfully created a reason, however arbitrary, to go to war.

Predictably, the Sioux under Sitting Bull could not meet the requirements of the ultimatum, and the U.S. attacked. Beginning in May 1876, American forces swept through the Black Hills trying to drive the Sioux back on their reservation and pressure Sioux leadership in to selling their land.

The initial phase of this operation was a colossal failure by the United States. In Mid-June, Crazy Horse and his men defeated an American force at Rosebud, and forced them to retreat. Just more than one week later, the Americans suffered what many consider to be the worst defeat in U.S. military history.

On June 25, 1876, George Armstrong Custer led his troops on a campaign to attack an Indian settlement along the Little Bighorn River, which is located in present day Montana. As Custer moved through the ravines and hidden channels of the Black Hills, he divided his army in order to gain a strategic advantage over the natives. This would prove to be a fatal mistake.

Custer had earned the reputation of being a risky, aggressive commander. This fighting strategy had served him well in the Civil War, but would ultimately be his downfall at Little Bighorn. Hugely outnumbered and with a divided force, Custer launched an attack against the Sioux camp, but failed when his horses could not cross the Little Bighorn River. With his attack stalled, he had been left vulnerable to a counter-attack by the Sioux.

Custer retreated to a nearby hill, now known as "Last Stand Hill." He and his small band of men were completely surrounded by a massive circle of Sioux warriors on horses closing in.

The Americans under General Custer were completely and totally defeated. Their last chance rested with other American forces, who were miles away, and would ultimately not make it in time. Around fifty men fought and died alongside Custer in what is now known as "Custer's Last Stand." In all, over two hundred and fifty men died in the Battle of Little Bighorn, in what was a resounding victory for the Sioux.

The Battle of Little Bighorn was arguably the worst military defeat in American History, though the U.S. was able to salvage some good out of the embarrassment. The narrative that came from Little Bighorn was the heroism of Custer, staying and fighting to the last against the savage

Sioux enemy. This battle was easily propagandized to highlight both the American valor and the Indian barbarism that the Great Sioux War had come to represent. Custer's last stand became a symbol and rallying cry for Americans to renew their dedication to taking the Black Hills from the Sioux.

The American troops were back in the Black Hills in 1877. This new campaign was much more successful for the larger and more technologically advanced United States. Crazy Horse surrendered and was captured in May, and killed under somewhat mysterious circumstances later that year.

The Sioux were continually beaten back, and Sitting Bull was forced to flee to Canada. In 1877, the U.S. officially annexed and occupied the Great Sioux Reservation. The permanent homeland that Red Cloud had won so brilliantly, did not even last a decade.

With the Sioux mostly defeated in 1877, a new era of Native American life began. Tribes were now reduced to living on small, undesirable reservations of land. These reservations would prevent them from effectively farming or hunting, and in essence completely robbed them of their previous way of life.

Natives had long been severely outnumbered and outgunned by the Americans, but now the discrepancy was so large that even the most optimistic of native leaders must have seen that any resistance to the United States was hopeless.

For Americans, the threat of Native Americans had never been lower. By hook or by crook, they had effectively ended the threat that natives had posed to American progress. However, the long tradition of violence against Native Americans tragically still had one more bloody chapter.

Chapter Six
Massacre

The 1880's represented a grim time for what was left of the Native Americans. By this point in time, the vast majority of Native American culture had been destroyed. Death by disease, murder, and war had wiped out millions over the centuries.

Millions more had assimilated to "white" culture, and while some kept elements of their ancestral heritage alive, much of it was lost to memory, and would eventually die out as generations passed. Even the legendary chief Geronimo succumbed to the unstoppable encroachment of the U.S., and surrendered to the army in 1886.

For the Native Americans that clung to their tradition and culture on the reservations, life was difficult. Just as it was in the years leading up to Little Bighorn, the reservations were extremely reliant on Americans for survival. Reservations were deprived of natural resources and were often exceedingly poor. The "Indian problem" for the United States had, for all intents and purposes, been solved.

Americans had certainly shifted their attitudes and beliefs about Native Americans. The U.S. had proved that they were the dominant force on the continent. Many had lingering questions, perhaps even guilt, about the debatable morality of their choices to destroy Native Americans. Many more were enraged by Indian barbarism against their heroic General Custer.

One of the villains in the Custer story was Sitting Bull, who had fled to Canada in 1877, after the U.S. occupied the Sioux reservation. Sitting Bull returned to the U.S. in 1881, and surrendered to the U.S. government. He was officially taken as a prisoner of war upon his return, but by 1886, he returned to the Standing Rock reservation to live with his people under the close watch of the U.S. government.

With the culture of the Native Americans dwindling and being painfully appropriated by the United States, the tragic story of American domination over the natives could have been written off as complete. Unfortunately for both sides, the tragedy was not yet finished. The year 1890 saw more bloodshed brought about by fear, misunderstanding, and distrust. The terrible cycle that had begun in Jamestown was about to take another spin.

The Ghost Dance

On January 1, 1889, a Paiute Indian named Wovoka had a fantastic dream. This night, he dreamed that the white man would be expelled from the Earth. After they were gone, the buffalo population would be restored, and every dead Native American would come back to earth and live amongst their ancestors in their old homelands.

Life would return to that time when Native Americans ruled the continent, before the arrival of the Europeans, and they would be happy and free of fear. In short, Wovoka imagined the absolute best-case fantasy scenario for the Native American peoples. He believed that in order for this dream to become a reality, he must spread the word and teach people the "Ghost Dance."

The Ghost Dance had started in the 1870's, but at that time it was only practiced by a few tribes in what is now Nevada—far west of the Sioux territory. The dance required people to move in a continuous circle pattern to a specific drum beat. This particular version of the dance incorporated the continuous circle element, but also encouraged people to work themselves into a kind of spiritual frenzy. Once all these elements were present, the key to success was to dance on a regimented schedule. Wovoka told the chiefs:

> *"When you get home you must begin a dance and continue for five days. Dance for four successive nights, and on the last night continue dancing until the morning of the fifth day, when all must bathe in the river and then return to their homes. You must all do this in the same way... I want you to dance every six weeks. Make a feast at the dance and have food that everybody may eat."*

Eventually, Wovoka believed, they could dance this dream of his into existence, and reestablish their culture to its former glory. Wovoka had become "the prophet," and to Native Americans, a possible messiah that would deliver them from their suffering.

Word spread quickly of Wovoka's vision. Thousands of chiefs traveled to Nevada to learn the dance and take it back to their tribes. Wovoka instructed these chiefs to keep the reason for the dance a secret from the Americans.

While understandable, this was quite alarming. Americans were fearful of this new, invigorating, and secretive movement that seemed to be unifying tribes. What's more, they heard about the fanatical behavior of this new dance, which was also unsettling. From a distrustful American perspective, it is easy to see why they were concerned about renewed violence.

For Native Americans, this was a chance, however slim, to live in the paradise that to this point, had been a pure imagination. It is likely that for years, natives had longed for a return to the time before Europeans, and wished and hoped for the kind of miracle that Wovoka had seen in his dream. They *wanted* to believe, and they attempted to dance this fantasy in to reality. Perhaps, they prayed, by some miracle, the Ghost Dance would work.

While the natives danced, the Americans were growing nervous. Nervous soldiers are more accident prone, and tend to be a recipe for disaster.

Wounded Knee

For the Sioux, the Ghost Dance took on a particularly militaristic hue. Natives believed that the dance had put a spell on their shirts, and had turned them into bulletproof "ghost shirts."

The Sioux were not as secretive as other tribes, and talked openly about this day of reckoning, where they would once again be masters of the continent. To an uninformed outsider, the behavior of the Sioux made it appear they hungered for war, and battle may be on the horizon.

Not helping to lower tensions, Sitting Bull had allowed his tribe to participate in the Ghost Dance. This was another red flag for the Americans, given that Sitting Bull had once before been a successful commander of Indian forces.

The U.S. government agent on the reservation did not know what Sitting Bull's next move would be, so they decided to make the first move. On December 15, 1890, a group of around forty reservation policemen went to arrest Sitting Bull. They surrounded his house, and ordered him to come back with them to the station. Sitting Bull refused. When he refused, the police used force and dragged Sitting Bull out of his house.

Due to this use of force against Sitting Bull, the Sioux people reacted. A Sioux warrior fired his rifle at a policeman, which delved the situation in to murderous chaos. The policemen who were arresting Sitting Bull shot him; getting him in the chest and the head.

Perhaps the greatest Indian leader of his age was unceremoniously murdered in front of his own people. His death caused open fire to erupt on both sides. When the dust settled, eight policemen and seven Natives, including Sitting Bull, were dead.

The natives, all too familiar with this kind of situation, knew they were no longer safe on their reservation. The Americans would be back for revenge. They needed to leave. Some two hundred Lakota Sioux, now leaderless, fled to join a nearby chief at the neighboring Pine Ridge Reservation—in present day South Dakota. When hearing about the bloodshed, the Americans decided they needed to disarm the Sioux and thus eliminate the threat of this Ghost Dance. Tensions had become explosively high.

On December 29, 1890, a U.S. Army group of nearly five hundred men approached a group of around three hundred and fifty Sioux—two thirds of which were women and children—at Wounded Knee Creek, in present day South Dakota.

Both sides were incredibly jumpy, given the violent outbreak of just two weeks prior. The American soldiers demanded the Sioux hand over their weapons. Nervously, the Sioux complied. American soldiers began searching homes and taking the weapons they found.

What happens next will never be known and is still widely debated to this day. Witnesses say one deaf Sioux warrior did not understand the order he had been given, and was not giving up his rifle. Two on-edge American soldiers grabbed this warrior from behind, and the rifle went off. It is unclear whether this first shot was accidental, the result of a scuffle for control of the weapon, or if it was an attack. Regardless, a shot being fired caused these nervous tensions to boil over.

American soldiers opened fire on the mostly unarmed Sioux in the camp, slaughtering them in great number. The remaining Sioux scattered. Sioux warriors went for their weapons to fight back, but many of them could not get there in time before being cut down. Women and children ran for their lives. Complete chaos erupted at Wounded Knee.

American soldiers continued firing ferociously at the Sioux, even targeting the unarmed women and children. As American Horse, an eyewitness to the carnage said:

> *"Right near the flag of truce a mother was shot down with her infant; the child not knowing that its mother was dead was still nursing, and that especially was a very sad sight. The women as they were fleeing with their babes were killed together, shot right through, and the women who were very heavy with child were also killed. All the Indians fled in three directions, and after most all of them had been killed, a cry was made that all those who were not killed or wounded should come forth and they would be safe. Little boys who were not wounded came out of their places of refuge, and as soon as they came in sight a number of soldiers surrounded them and butchered them there."*

The American soldiers had lost all semblance of discipline. They were butchering civilians. They killed wounded Sioux, and hunted down the Sioux that had run away. Another observer, Turning Hawk, describes the scene of the ravine next to the camp:

"...those who escaped that first fire got into the ravine, and as they went along up the ravine for a long distance they were pursued on both sides by the soldiers and shot down, as the dead bodies showed afterwards. The women were standing off at a different place form where the men were stationed, and when the firing began, those of the men who escaped the first onslaught went in one direction up the ravine, and then the women, who were bunched together at another place, went entirely in a different direction through an open field, and the women fared the same fate as the men who went up the deep ravine."

When the firing finally stopped, somewhere between two hundred and three hundred Sioux lay dead. Twenty-five American soldiers had been killed.

The Wounded Knee Massacre drove a stake through heart of Native American culture and memory. The pipe dream of the Ghost Dance was gone. Native Americans were more oppressed than they had ever been, their people and their traditions crushed. Americans had proven again they were capable of the kind of savagery and barbarism they had so long accused the natives of.

To add insult to injury, the United States awarded twenty American soldiers the Congressional Medal of Honor, the highest honor possible in the U.S. military, for their heroism and courage at Wounded Knee. Many Americans celebrated the news from Wounded Knee as another great victory for the U.S. Army. Others decried it as the massacre that it was. Regardless, Wounded Knee has become the lasting image for both Native Americans and Americans to the conflict and violence between these two groups.

Wounded Knee is in many ways, a perfect microcosm of the entire relationship between Native Americans and the United States. Both sides were shackled by fear, ignorance, mistrust, and miscommunication. Mistakes were made out of haste, carelessness, and nervousness.

Wounded Knee was the result of another failed attempt at diplomacy and another nasty example of the pattern of violence that neither side could avoid. Of all the tragic moments in this story, it is Wounded Knee that endures in our historical memory as the true moment of anguish. Americans have arguably never looked worse than they did on December 29, 1890. That day also represents a day of utter defeat, in every sense of the word, for Native Americans.

In 1927, American poet Stephen Vincent Benet, perhaps unintentionally, captured the essence of what Wounded Knee meant and still means to the Native Americans. In the closing verse of his poem entitled *American Names,* Benet writes:

I shall not be there. I shall rise and pass.

Bury my heart at Wounded Knee.

Chapter Seven

Kill the Indian, Save the Man

Just two years after the Wounded Knee Massacre, Colonel Richard Henry Pratt, the founder of the famous Carlisle Indian Boarding School, famously said:

> *"A great general has said that the only good Indian is a dead one, and that high sanction of his destruction has been an enormous factor in promoting Indian massacres. In a sense, I agree with the sentiment, but only in this: that all the Indian there is in the race should be dead. Kill the Indian in him, and save the man."*

Beginning in the 1880's, the United States adopted a new solution to their long-standing "Indian problem." Looking for a solution to the centuries of violence, the government turned to what they considered to be peaceful solutions: education and total assimilation.

The U.S. government believed the natives could adopt the "white" lifestyle, which would eventually erode and erase Indian culture and heritage. By adopting "whiteness," the U.S. would "kill" what made someone an Indian, without having to actually kill the person. This line of thinking was prejudiced, flawed, and had devastating results on Native American communities.

The Dawes Act

The year 1887 saw the passage of the Dawes Act, which allowed the U.S. government to divide up Indian land and give it to individual Native Americans who chose to live like "the white man" and renounced their tribal membership.

In return, Native Americans who chose to leave their tribe would privately own land and be given a path to U.S. citizenship. The U.S. government was incentivizing individual natives to leave their tribes and cultures.

Henry Dawes, a Massachusetts Senator and the author of the bill, saw this as a way to save Native Americans, while also obtaining valuable land for the United States. Dawes believed that Indians must assimilate, or they would eventually die under the expansion of U.S. railroad and mining interests. This was a way for the U.S. to remove themselves from their perceived paternal role over the Native American tribes, and empower Native Americans to have individual economic self-sufficiency.

Predictably, the Dawes Act did not turn out like Henry Dawes had envisioned. Even more predictably, the United States ended up benefitting greatly from the act, while Native Americans were once again on the losing side of the bargain.

Many Native Americans took the deal offered to them by the Dawes Act, and obtained individual parcels of land. In many cases, these lands were not suitable farm lands and could realistically never become profitable. In many other cases, the natives who were given the land did not have the necessary tools and equipment or the money to buy the necessary tools and equipment in order to be successful.

Natives were inexperienced with this type of agriculture and lifestyle, so they made mistakes, which would ultimately doom them financially. To add another challenge, when the original Indian land holder died, the land was divided between their heirs. This segmented the already poor land into even smaller parcels with even more owners. The conditions that existed made economic self-sufficiency extremely difficult to obtain. The barriers to success for most natives were too much to overcome, so they turned to the obvious solution; sell the land.

Ultimately, this is what they did. Native Americans sold their Dawes Act land en masse, and often sold it for pennies on the dollar. They sold it back to the U.S. government, who in turn built on the land. They sold it to corporations, like the railroad companies, who had other uses for the land that was profitable. They sold it to Americans that had the capital and equipment to successfully farm the land if it was suitable.

Over the next fifty years, Native Americans would sell ninety million acres of land, which was around sixty percent of all native held land in the U.S. Thousands of Native Americans had just sold their greatest asset, and were left with few options to combat the massive poverty they now found themselves in.

The Dawes Act was a crippling political tool of assimilation that devastated Native American culture, and in many ways created the conditions that many Native

American communities struggle with today. The United States ended up achieving their desired bottom line. They got the land they wanted, but it did come at yet another great moral cost.

Boarding Schools

In addition to the Dawes Act, the U.S. turned to another "peaceful" tool of assimilation; education. Beginning in the 1880s, the U.S. government created boarding schools where native children would be taken away from their homes and immersed in a white American education.

As Richard Henry Pratt put it, they could "kill the Indian" by killing a child's native culture, language, religion, and traditions and "save the man," by replacing those things with white culture and traditions. Pratt believed this would be a bloodless, cultural takeover of the Indian youth, and would replace killing on the battlefield.

Assimilation had been tried many times before, but the 1880s, with Dawes Act and boarding schools, was by far the most systematic and widespread attempt at folding natives into "white" culture. Pratt had opened the well-known Carlisle Indian Boarding School in Pennsylvania in 1879, which became the model for several other federally operated Indian schools.

By 1902, there were twenty-five such schools that served over six thousand Native American students. By 1973, over sixty thousand Native American children were in the boarding school system. While they began to decline in the late 1970s, the schools lasted well in to the twentieth century, the last ones closing in the 1990s.

The schools are perhaps the most direct attempt at ethnic cleansing in United States history. Children from all tribes were ripped away from their families and sent hundreds, sometimes even thousands of miles away from their homes to these schools. They often stayed at these schools for years and rarely, if ever, saw their families. They were forced to speak English, and were punished if they spoke in their native languages. They were taught to practice Christianity, and were not given the freedom to practice their own religions.

Their traditional Native American long hair was cut in to contemporary "white" hair styles. They were made to wear military-style uniforms instead of their traditional tribal clothing. They were frequently made to take white,

"Christian" names to use at school and would not be allowed to use their given names.

Essentially, the schools attempted to strip away any sort of Native American cultural identity and make these children "white." The boarding schools were designed to kill Indian culture and solve the Indian problem once and for all.

Conditions at these schools were often unthinkably poor. Students were severely punished for breaking the rules, often physically abused for crimes like attempting to speak their native tongue or worship their religion.

At Haskell, a school in Lawrence, KS, a solitary confinement jail cell was used for misbehaving students, complete with child-sized handcuffs. Students would be there sometimes for days on end. Sanitary conditions were also poor, as sickness and disease ran rampant through the school population.

In addition to the physical conditions, emotional and sexual abuse was also suffered by the native children. As a result of these poor conditions, a number of students died while attending these forced assimilation schools. At places like Carlisle and Haskell, it was necessary to build cemeteries on campus for these students who died under the schools "care," while isolated from their homes and families.

While the battles and violent events like Wounded Knee capture the most historical attention, the boarding schools are perhaps the most tragic and vile chapter in the relationship between the U.S. and the Native Americans. It is bad enough that these schools were created to kill native culture and tradition. But to execute that shameful plan while abusing children, to the point of death in some cases, is unconscionable.

While it looks very different than the atrocities of the past, the common thread of American ethno-centrism and racism underlies the tragedy of the Indian Boarding School.

As Native American and historian David Treuer said, "Education was something done *to* us, not something provided *for* us."

For all the effort the United States put forth to "kill the Indian," these schools were largely unsuccessful. In many cases, the schools had the opposite of the intended effect.

Native children clung even tighter to their traditions and cultures, bonded with children from other tribes, and showed a proud resiliency that has come to define Native American culture today.

To the Present

In many ways, the U.S. was fortunate that boarding schools were ineffective. The sustained life and usage of Native American languages became very useful for the American military in both World War I and World War II.

The U.S. military recruited native speakers, most famously the Navajo, to send coded messages that would be undecipherable by the enemy. The well-known "Navajo Code Talkers" played a critical role in the American campaign against Japan in the Pacific theater of World War II, contributing greatly to American victory on Iwo-Jima. Luckily for those marines on Iwo-Jima, the boarding schools did not kill the Navajo language like they had attempted.

Native Americans continued to fight for equal rights and treatment through the civil rights movement of the 1960s. In 1968, the U.S. Congress passed the *Indian Civil Rights Act* which clearly defined native rights and extended some, but not all, powers from the Bill of Rights in the U.S. Constitution to the Native Americans. More significant was the *1975 Indian Self-Determination and Education*

Assistance Act, which expanded the power of tribal governments and allowed Native Americans to create and run schools on their own.

Taking ownership of schools was a key step in protecting and preserving what remains of native culture. Tribes can now teach their children according to their traditions and beliefs, and continue the study of native languages.

In 1980, the Sioux finally won a prolonged legal battle with the United States. The Sioux had long believed that the U.S. seizing of their reservation after Little Bighorn in 1877 was illegal and in violation of the treaty that they had signed. The Sioux took the U.S. government to court, and in 1980, the Supreme Court ruled in their favor.

The Supreme Court ruled that the U.S. illegally took the land, and awarded compensation to the Sioux for their property being taken.

Supreme Court Justice Harry Blackmun wrote in the decision that: "A more ripe and rank case of dishonorable dealings will never, in all probability, be found in our history"

Today, the U.S. government owes the Sioux over a billion dollars to compensate them for their lost land. Out of principle, the Sioux, many of whom are impoverished, have refused this money for the last forty years. They remain firm in their position. They do not want to sell their land; they want to return to their land. For the Sioux, the fight continues.

The historical reverberations of the Dawes Act, the boarding schools and the violence in the late nineteenth century are still being felt very strongly by Native Americans today. While the Americans did not kill native culture like they had intended, many natives were caught between two cultures and did not feel fully like a member of either one.

Natives would have had hard time ever completely assimilating into American culture, because they were not white. Even if they adopted every American custom, their racial and ethnic background would maintain their status as "second class citizens." While they were unsuccessfully being turned "white" on their parcel of land or at their boarding school, they were losing critical parts of their heritage.

Children at boarding schools had been wrenched away from their families during critical childhood years, and lost a piece of their tradition they could never regain. Natives who attempted to assimilate would never fit back in to the traditional native culture that belonged to their parents and grandparents. This cultural identity crisis has had profound negative impacts on Native American survival and self-esteem.

The long history of trauma, loss, and conquest has created a situation where today, many Native American communities are crippled by poverty, drug, and alcohol abuse, and high rates of mental illnesses like depression and anxiety. These problems are multi-faceted and complicated challenges that threaten the well-being of numerous Native Americans.

Despite being under attack for four hundred years and now being threatened by a new kind of enemy, Native American culture and traditions still survive. They have overcome the gradual erosion of their heritage, the loss of their land and resources, and the death of most of their people. Still, they endure. Native Americans have lost more than anyone could ever imagine, but they did not lose their pride or their resiliency.

The Native Americans have always been a proud and amazingly resilient people, and these traits have carried what remains of their culture in to the present day.

Chapter Eight

The Noble Savage

One area where conflict between Native Americans and Americans still exists is in the battle for memory. Americans have a strange and complicated relationship with the historical memory and culture of Native Americans.

A critical moment in this battle for historical memory occurred during the 1880s. After his re-capture and before his return to the reservation, Sitting Bull, the legendary and important leader of the Sioux, was making money as a regular member of the *Buffalo Bill Cody Wild West Show*. Sitting Bull would ride in as a main attraction to the delight of audiences. He and Buffalo Bill Cody even had a picture together that read: "Sitting Bull and Buffalo Bill: Foes in 76—Friends in 85." This is both a very strange and very sad statement about the status of Native American culture in the American mind.

Scarce in history are there examples of a vanquished "enemy" leader like Sitting Bull, who once dealt a crushing military blow to the U.S.—Little Bighorn—being *voluntarily* paraded around as a glorified prop less than decade after the fighting stopped.

This was not a Roman triumphal parade where the vanquished foe was publicly spit on, humiliated, and panned by their conquerors. This was a genuine fascination; an entertainment attraction for Americans. This fact illustrates the unusual memory that Americans have created surrounding Indians. When Sitting Bull rode in Buffalo Bill Cody's show, the myth of the modern "wild west" was beginning to take shape.

The idea of the "wild west" has long been part of American folklore, and the Indians on the plains are a big part of that story. The image that has been crafted to fit that mythology of the west is one of the *noble savage*.

Since the natives had not been civilized, they were close to living in the true "state of nature," which both exposed their intrinsic virtue and also their inherent backwards-ness.

Americans like to think of Native Americans, like Sitting Bull, or Tecumseh before him, as crude, not technologically advanced, and capable of barbarism, while at the same time being honorable men, fighting for the defense of their homes, their people, and their way of life: A *noble* cause, for a *savage* being.

This idea of the *noble savage* has created a nostalgia around Native Americans that still very much exists in American culture. For years, movie stars like John Wayne played heroic cowboys fighting against these noble savages in iconic American western movies.

Media like this has shaped American beliefs about the "wild west," but also cemented the ideas of the "noble savage" to new generations of Americans. This view of the "wild west" is so popular and nostalgic that generations of American children have played "cowboys and Indians" in their backyards and in their video games.

This created myth has seeped in to American historical memory and shaped American beliefs about a people and culture. These beliefs are inaccurate, incomplete, and narrow. Ultimately, American popular culture has been very damaging to the understanding and acceptance of Native American culture.

Today, the most visible example of this "noble savage" ideology is the bevy of sports teams and mascots that are named after or reference Native Americans. Secondary schools, colleges, and professional teams across the United States compete with logos, mascots, and traditions that are walking examples of the "noble savage."

Teams and their fans want to identify with both the "Indian ferocity" of combat, but also with the sincerity and nobility of their cause. Native Americans and their culture are being appropriated, often portrayed as being cartoonish, bloodthirsty, and barbaric. While there are some cases where Native American mascots are honorific and agreed upon by the local tribes, many Native Americans find the use of their culture and symbols in this context to be offensive.

Some of the mascots have been quite controversial in recent years, and the attention that this issue is getting may signal a shift in American views about Native Americans and their culture is on the horizon.

Regardless, the very existence of these mascots illustrates the American mindset toward Native Americans that has existed since Sitting Bull appeared on the *Buffalo Bill Cody Wild West Show*. The mindset is rooted in the belief that natives are on some level inferior—after all, the majority of sports mascots are animals, so the fact that native culture is grouped similarly should be telling.

Americans have a unique enthrallment for a people that they tried to destroy repeatedly throughout their history. This is a bit different than the typical romanticism of the past. History is often exaggerated, the truth stretched, to best serve whoever is telling the story. That romanticism has undoubtedly occurred in this story, but something else has also occurred.

Native Americans hold a unique place in American cultural memory. They sit somewhere between mythical, villainous, and tragically heroic all at the same time. They somehow can be considered both enemies and friends. They are revered, yet rejected. No other group holds this paradoxical of a place in American historical memory.

Conclusion

The American Indian Wars is among the worst tragedies in American history. On one hand, the story is simple. Two vastly different cultures clash, one with far superior technology, and they begin to compete over the same resources. Both sides are plagued by fear, prejudice, greed, and the instinct of self-preservation.

When these realities interact, violence, death, and tragedy often are the outcome. It is not hard to understand why the Americans were so successful in this conflict, or why the conflict began in the first place. What is not so simple are the underlying truths behind the American Indian Wars.

What was the meaning of this conflict? What does it say about America and American identity? What does it say about Native Americans? These are extremely complicated, difficult, and controversial questions even today.

The history of any nation is filled with both triumph and tragedy. In many cases, a nation's history can be a burden and weigh heavily on the minds, memories, and self-esteem of a people.

The American Indian Wars carry a tremendous amount of historical weight for both cultures. Memory has contributed to the problems facing Native American communities today, and also serves as a painful motivator and reminder to preserve their heritage.

Native Americans, resiliently and bravely, still survive, yet as a distant, almost unrecognizable shell of what their nation used to be. The weight of history bears such a heavy burden on Native Americans that there are few—if any—surviving cultures that have to wear such a substantial and grim coat on their shoulders. There should be no mistaking that Native Americans bear the overwhelming majority of the weight of this tragic past.

Memory has also called in to question the legitimacy of core American values like equality and self-government. It has also infused American history, for some, with a certain degree of guilt. For the United States, the history with the Native Americans is one of the starkest examples of classic American paradox.

From an American perspective, all of the decisions that were made by the government were to help the United States. Gaining resources, land, safety, and power were clear positives for Americans, and the decision-makers were willing to see American progress occur at the expense of the Native Americans.

This is the crux of the fascinating and vexing paradox that underlies the U.S. during this story. American progress, which is good and true, served as the engine for genocide, which is abhorrent, but also true. It is difficult for our modern society to accept two seemingly opposite things both being true at the same time, but that is exactly what this story requires.

While many Americans are ashamed of the atrocities that their country committed against the Indians, they are also proud that America went on to fulfill her grand destiny and ultimately became the most powerful nation on earth.

Should Americans feel pride for their historical accomplishments, or regret for their historical mistakes? The answer is both, which is problematic because it is a complete contradiction. The difficulty in reconciling these two conflicting truths is the force that drives the paradox in American historical memory.

If one can accept that both things are true: that America is both right and wrong at the same time, it begs an even deeper question about this tortured relationship. Was this tragedy inevitable? Was it a necessary tragedy in order for America to reach the heights that it did?

It is easy to dismiss any question of historical inevitability as being incorrect. For any historical event, including the American Indian Wars, there are hundreds of moments, actions, and decisions that shaped and altered the outcome of the story. Change the outcome of just one, and the entire event plays out differently than it did.

Answers refuting the inevitability of a certain event are numerous and easy to find in this story. However, a compelling argument can be made for the inevitability of this tragedy. Would Americans ever let Native Americans live on the land according to native customs and traditions? That seems very unlikely, given the nature of American land attitude and how natives were perceived as wasting that precious resource.

If Americans, philosophically, would never accept Native American land use, which is a very plausible, even likely, estimation, then war between the two sides starts to appear inevitable. What other solution could be found?

Despite some periods of peace, the two cultures were simply incompatible. Perhaps cultures with such different beliefs cannot coexist on the same land. This is not to excuse or justify American behavior toward the natives, but it does shed light on American thinking at decision-making through the course of the entire story.

An even more challenging question for Americans— was the U.S. conquest of the Native Americans necessary? Would America be the world super power that it is today if it had not been for the domination of their continent? There is no certain answer, but it is very reasonable to acknowledge the dependency of one outcome on the other.

Many would argue that America does not reach the power and success that she has had without the unfortunate conquest of the natives. Does that justify their actions? Was conquest a necessary evil on the road to American "manifest destiny?" Should the U.S. act honorably, even if it ultimately makes them weaker?

The wheel of paradox continues to revolve until one arrives at an even more difficult question. Is the purpose of a nation to reach its full potential for achievement? Or is it to selflessly govern and maintain peace, even at the expense of one's own national progress?

The answers to all of these questions will undoubtedly shape one's opinion and memory of the American Indian Wars. This story is unquestionably a tragedy, but it is not just a tragedy for its own sake. This conflict exposes something about the nature of civilization itself, and what happens when a group interferes with the relentless march of progress.

The past teaches lessons that can be applied to the present or future. Perhaps the lesson the American Indian Wars teaches is that tragedy is inevitable, even necessary, for the ultimate progress of civilization. Is that acceptable? Can we live with that truth? Do we even have a choice?

References

American Rhetoric (2017) Speech of Chief Tecumseh. Retrieved from: https://americanrhetoric.com/speeches/nativeamericans/chieftecumseh.htm

Baird, David (1973). "The Choctaws Meet the Americans, 1783 to 1843." *The Choctaw People*. United States: Indian Tribal Series.

Barbash, F & Elkind, P (1980). *Sioux win $105 Million*. The Washington Post (July 1, 1980). Retrieved from: https://www.washingtonpost.com/archive/politics/1980/07/01/sioux-win-105-million/a595cc88-36c6-49b9-be4f-6ea3c2a8fa06/?utm_term=.c70dcf06db63

Barret, Carole (2011) Encyclopedia of the Great Plains: Sioux Wars. Retrieved from http://plainshumanities.unl.edu/encyclopedia/doc/egp.war.044

BBC Documentary (2019) *The Wild West: Custer's Last Stand*. Retrieved from: https://www.youtube.com/watch?v=YPjTFXpAZ_g

Brown, Dee (1970) *Bury my heart at Wounded Knee*. New York, Holt, Rinehart & Winston

Burnett, John (1890) The Cherokee Removal Through the Eyes of a Private Soldier. Retrieved from https://www.warrenhills.org/cms/lib/NJ01001092/Centricity/Domain/145/Cherokee%20Removal%20through%20Eyes%20of%20a%20Private%20Soldier.pdf

Carlisle Indian School (2019) "1892 Speech of Richard H Pratt." Retrieved from: http://carlisleindian.dickinson.edu/teach/kill-indian-and-save-man-capt-richard-h-pratt-education-native-americans

Carter, John (2011) Encyclopedia of the Great Plains: Wounded Knee Massacre. Retrieved from: http://plainshumanities.unl.edu/encyclopedia/doc/egp.war.056

Columbus, Christopher (1492) "Diaries of Christopher Columbus." University of Gronigan (2012) *American History from Revolution to Reconstruction: Extracts from the Journal of Columbus.* Retrieved from http://www.let.rug.nl/usa/documents/before-1600/extracts-from-the-journal-of-columbus.php

Cray Jr., Robert (2009) Weltering in Their Own Blood: Puritan Casualties in King Philips War. Historical Journal of Massachusetts, Fall 2009 P 107-123

Cubbison, Douglas (2016) *The Grattan Fight: Prelude to a Generation of War.* Wyoming State Historical Society, Retrieved from: https://www.wyohistory.org/encyclopedia/grattan-fight-prelude-generation-war

Dixon, David (2005) *Never Come to Peace Again; Pontiac's Uprising and the fate of the British Empire in North America.* Norman, University of Oklahoma Press

Dunbar, W and May, G (1995). *Michigan: A History of the Wolverine State.* Grand Rapids: Eerdmans Publishing Company

Encyclopedia Britannica (2019) Metacom. Retrieved from https://www.britannica.com/biography/Metacom

Frank, Andrew (2019) "Five Civilized Tribes," *The Encyclopedia of Oklahoma History and Culture,* Retrieved from: https://www.okhistory.org/publications/enc/entry.php?entry=FI011

Frank, Andrew (2019) "Trail of Tears" *The Encyclopedia of Oklahoma History and Culture,* Retrieved from: https://www.okhistory.org/publications/enc/entry.php?entry=TR003

Gilbert, Bil (1995) *The Dying Tecumseh and the Birth of a Legend.* Smithsonian Magazine, July 1995. Retrieved from:

https://www.smithsonianmag.com/history/the-dying-tecumseh-97830806/

Griske, Michael (2005). *The Diaries of John Hunton.* Westminster, MD: Heritage Books.

History Channel (2019) Trail of Tears. Retrieved from: https://www.history.com/topics/native-american-history/trail-of-tears

Jackson, Donald, (1966) *Custer's Gold: The United States Cavalry Expedition of 1874*, New Haven

Jefferson, Thomas (1803) Instructions for Meriwhether Lewis. *Library of Congress* Retrieved from https://www.loc.gov/exhibits/lewisandclark/transcript57.html

Kerstetter, Todd (2011) Encyclopedia of the Great Plains: Ghost Dance. Retrieved from http://plainshumanities.unl.edu/encyclopedia/doc/egp.rel.023

Langguth, AJ (2006). *Union 1812: The Americans Who Fought the Second War of Independence.* New York: Simon and Schuster

Legends of America (2019) Ghost Dance. Retrieved from https://www.legendsofamerica.com/na-ghostdance/

Lepore, Jill (2018) *These Truths: A history of the United States.* New York, WW Norton & Co

Mahon, John K. (1967) *History of the Second Seminole War.* Gainesville, Florida: University of Florida Press

Mass Moments (2019) King Philips War Breaks Out. Retrieved from https://www.massmoments.org/moment-details/king-philips-war-breaks-out.html

Miller, Michael G. (2011) *"Red Cloud's War: An Insurgency case Study for Modern Times,"* US Army War College, Carlisle Barracks, PA

Minnesota Historical Society (2019) The US Dakota War of 1862. Retrieved from https://www.usdakotawar.org/

Missal, John & Mary Lou (2004) *The Seminole Wars: America's Longest Indian Conflict*. University Press of Florida

Mount Vernon Ladies Association (2019) Pontiacs Rebellion. Retrieved from https://www.mountvernon.org/library/digitalhistory/digital-encyclopedia/article/pontiacs-rebellion/

Museum of the Cherokee Indian (2019) Trail of Tears. Retrieved from https://www.cherokeemuseum.org/archives/era/trail-of-tears

National Park Service (2019) Sand Creek Massacre Historic Site: Retrieved from https://www.nps.gov/sand/learn/historyculture/people.htm

National Park Service (2019) Trail of Tears: Stories. Retrieved from https://www.nps.gov/trte/learn/historyculture/stories.html

Nebraska State Historical Society (2004) Battle of the Blue Water. Retrieved from https://history.nebraska.gov/blog/marker-monday-battle-blue-water

Newcomb, Steven (2012) The 1887 Dawes Act: The US theft of 90 million acres of Indian Land. *Indian Country Today*. News Maven. Retrieved from https://newsmaven.io/indiancountrytoday/archive/the-1887-dawes-act-the-u-s-theft-of-90-million-acres-of-indian-land-mhhCiBXdrU-pUbgWKwpOaQ/

Our Documents Initiative (2019) *The Dawes Act*. Retrieved from: https://www.ourdocuments.gov/doc.php?flash=false&doc=50

PBS (2019) *American Experience: Sitting Bull* Retrieved from https://www.pbs.org/wgbh/americanexperience/features/oakley-sitting-bull/

PBS (2019) *Indian Removal:* Retrieved from: http://www.shoppbs.pbs.org/wgbh/aia/part4/4p2959.html

PBS (2001) *New Perspectives on the West: Wounded Knee*. Retrieved from https://www.pbs.org/weta/thewest/resources/archives/eight/wklakota.htm

PBS (2001) *New Perspectives on the West: The Dawes Act.* Retrieved from https://www.pbs.org/weta/thewest/resources/archives/eight/dawes.html

PBS (2019) *The War of 1812.* Retrieved from: http://www.pbs.org/wned/war-of-1812/classroom/intermediate/bundle-twigs/

PBS Documentary (2016) *Unspoken: America's Native American Boarding Schools.* Retrieved from: https://www.pbs.org/video/unspoken-americas-native-american-boarding-schools-oobt1r/

Rowling, Richard (2003) *My Daily Constitution Vol III: A Natural Law Perspective.* United States, Xilbris Corporation

Schupman, Edwin (2007) Native Words, Native Warriors. *National Museum of the American Indian.* Retrieved from: https://americanindian.si.edu/education/codetalkers/html/chapter3.html

Seattle (1855) "Letter to President Franklin Pierce" *Thus spoke Chief Seattle, a story of undocumented speech* Jerry Clark. Prologue Magazine (1985) Vol. 18, No1. National Archives. Retrieved from: https://www.archives.gov/publications/prologue/1985/spring/chief-seattle.html

Streshinsky, Maria (2011) Saying no to $1 Billion. *The Atlantic* (March 2011) Retrieved from: https://www.theatlantic.com/magazine/archive/2011/03/saying-no-to-1-billion/308380/

University of Michigan Library (2018) *Great Native American Chiefs: Geronimo.* Retrieved from https://www.lib.umich.edu/online-exhibits/exhibits/show/great-native-american-chiefs/group-of-native-american-chief/geronimo

Utley, Robert M. (2004). *"The Last Days of the Sioux Nation,* 2nd Edition." Yale University Press.

Virtual Jamestown (1998) *Robert Beverley's Description of the 1622 Indian Attack.* Retrieved from http://www.virtualjamestown.org/1622attk.html

Wong, Alia (2019) The Schools That Tried—But Failed—to Make Native Americans Obsolete. *The Atlantic*. Retrieved from: https://www.theatlantic.com/education/archive/2019/03/failed-assimilation-native-american-boarding-schools/584017/

About History Compacted

Here in History Compacted, we see history as a large collection of stories. Each of these amazing stories of the past can help spark ideas for the future. However, history is often proceeded as boring and incomprehensible. That is why it is our mission to simplify the fascinating stories of history.

Follow History Compacted:

Website: www.historycompacted.com

Twitter: @HistoryCompact

Facebook: https://www.facebook.com/historycompacted/

Dark Minds In History

For updates about new releases, as well as exclusive promotions, sign up for our newsletter and you can also receive a free book today. Thank you and see you soon.

Sign up here: http://bit.ly/2ToHti3

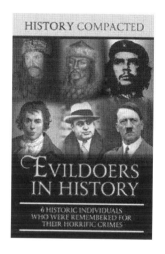

Evildoers in History: 6 Historic Individuals Remembered For Their Horrific Crimes is a book that explores the stories of six infamous criminals in history, these evildoers were not remembered by their countless murders but by the brutality with which they took the lives of their victims. There is no other term to describe them but ruthless, as you will soon find out.

Prepare yourself, the gruesome part of history is not for everyone...

Made in the USA
Lexington, KY
23 October 2019